Telling Time

Written by Ann H. Matzke

Rourke
Educational Media

rourkeeducationalmedia.com

Scan for Related Titles
and Teacher Resources

www.rourkeeducationalmedia.com

PHOTO CREDITS: Cover: © koosen; Title Page: © BartCo; Page 3: © JoseGirarte; Page 4: © Smitt; Page 5: © Arturo Peña Romano Medina; Page 6: © Brooklynworks; Page 7: © ElaineRich; Page 8: © Samuel Borges Photography; Page 9, 10, 11, 13, 18, 20, 22: © Mark Evans; Page 14: © Andrey Savin; Page 16: © Monkeybusinessimages; Page 17: © Crisma; Page 19: © Kali9; Page 21: © RBfried; Page 23: © Jianying Yin

Edited by Jill Sherman

Cover and Interior design by Tara Raymo

Library of Congress PCN Data

Telling Time / Ann H. Matzke
(Little World Math)
ISBN 978-1-62169-884-5 (hard cover)
ISBN 978-1-62169-779-4 (soft cover)
ISBN 978-1-62169-983-5 (e-Book)
Library of Congress Control Number: 2013936801

Also Available as:

Rourke Educational Media
Printed in the United States of America,
North Mankato, Minnesota

Rourke
Educational Media

rourkeeducationalmedia.com

customerservice@rourkeeducationalmedia.com • PO Box 643328 Vero Beach, Florida 32964

What time is it?

Long ago, people told time by nature.

They watched the changing seasons
and the Moon.

Ancient Egyptians used a shadow clock called a sundial.

Sundial

The Sun's shadow moved as time passed.

Modern-day Sundial

Modern clocks measure time in hours, minutes, and seconds.

The three hands move at different speeds.

The shortest hand, or hour hand, moves the slowest. It counts the hours.

The minute hand is longer and moves faster than the hour hand. It counts the minutes.

The second hand moves the fastest, circling in 60 seconds or one minute.

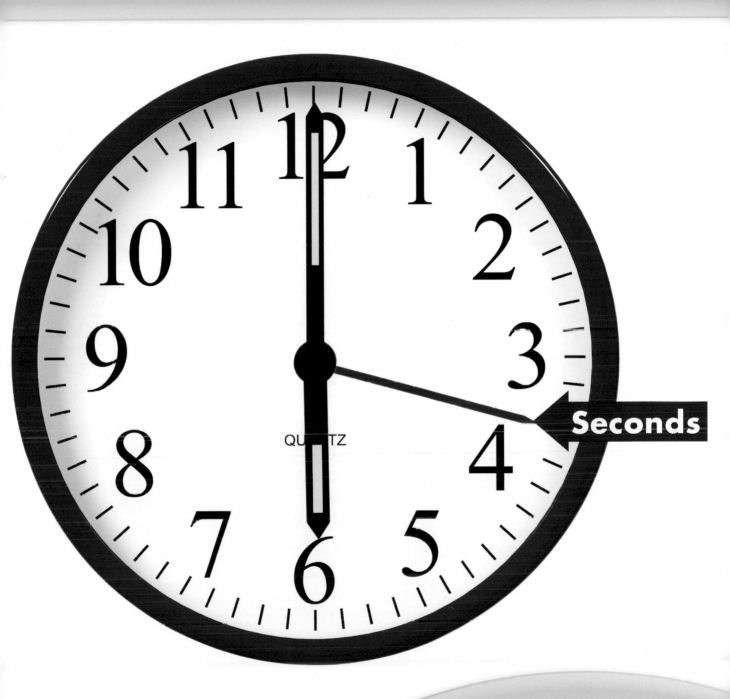

Seconds

Digital clocks do not use hands. They only show numbers. The numbers change as time passes.

The numbers to the left of the two dots tell the hour. The numbers to the right tell the minutes.

We tell time using a.m. for the time before noon.

We use p.m. for the afternoon
and nighttime.

Let's practice telling time. Which is the right time?

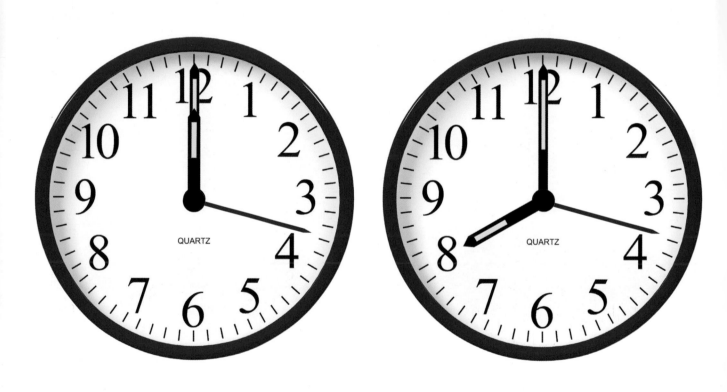

8:00 a.m. is the right time. It is time to go to school.

Which time is right?

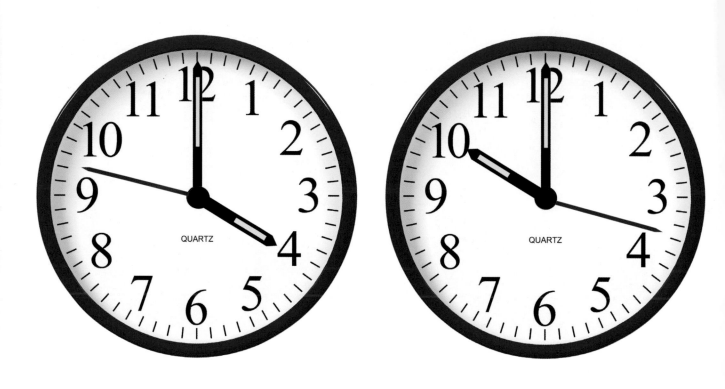

4:00 p.m. is the right time for a game after school!

Which time is right?

6:30 p.m. is the right time for dinner.
Telling time is alright!

Index

Websites

pbskids.org/cyberchase/videos/harrys-time-out
www.abcya.com/telling_time.htm
funschool.kaboose.com/formula-fusion/games/game_what_time_is_it.html

About the Author

Ann H. Matzke is a children's librarian. She has an MFA in Writing for Children and Young Adults from Hamline University. She lives with her family in Gothenburg, Nebraska. To pass the time she enjoys reading and writing books for children.

Meet The Author!
www.meetREMauthors.com